W9-CDI-807

DIRECTION, ALIGNMENT, COMMITMENT:
ACHIEVING BETTER RESULTS THROUGH LEADERSHIP

This series of books draws on the practical knowledge that the Center for Creative Leadership (CCL®) has generated, since its inception in 1970, through its research and educational activity conducted in partnership with hundreds of thousands of managers and executives. Much of this knowledge is shared—in a way that is distinct from the typical university department, professional association, or consultancy. CCL is not simply a collection of individual experts, although the individual credentials of its staff are impressive; rather it is a community, with its members holding certain principles in common and working together to understand and generate practical responses to today's leadership and organizational challenges.

The purpose of the series is to provide managers with specific advice on how to complete a developmental task or solve a leadership challenge. In doing that, the series carries out CCL's mission to advance the understanding, practice, and development of leadership for the benefit of society worldwide. We think you will find the Ideas Into Action Series an important addition to your leadership toolkit.

DIRECTION, ALIGNMENT, COMMITMENT:

ACHIEVING BETTER RESULTS THROUGH LEADERSHIP

CYNTHIA MCCAULEY
LYNN FICK-COOPER

Center for
Creative
Leadership·

IDEAS INTO ACTION SERIES

Aimed at managers and executives who are concerned with their own and others' development, each book in this series gives specific advice on how to complete a developmental task or solve a leadership problem.

LEAD CONTRIBUTORS
Cynthia McCauley
Lynn Fick-Cooper

CONTRIBUTORS
Janny Brust, Robert Burnside, Julie Willems Van Dijk, Bill Drath, David Horth, Lynn Miller, Harold Scharlatt, Preston Yarborough

DIRECTOR OF ASSESSMENTS, TOOLS, AND PUBLICATIONS
Sylvester Taylor

MANAGER, PUBLICATION DEVELOPMENT
Peter Scisco

EDITOR
Stephen Rush

ASSOCIATE EDITOR
Shaun Martin

DESIGN, LAYOUT, AND COVER DESIGN
Ed Morgan, navybluedesign.com

RIGHTS AND PERMISSIONS
Kelly Lombardino

EDITORIAL BOARD
David Altman, Elaine Bleich, Regina Eckert, Joan Gurvis, Jennifer Habig, Kevin Liu, Kelly Lombardino, Neal Maillet, Jennifer Martineau, Portia Mount, Laura Santana, Harold Scharlatt

CCL No. 00462

978-1-60491-553-2 - Print
978-1-60491-554-9 - Ebook

Center for Creative Leadership
www.ccl.org

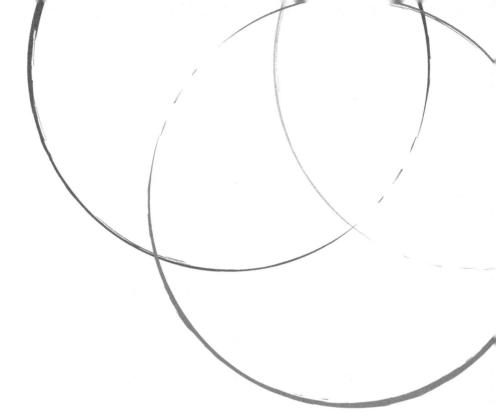

CONTENTS

DO YOU HAVE A LEADERSHIP PROBLEM?

Is your group getting results? Is it hitting targets, achieving quality standards, meeting deadlines, making timely decisions, or exceeding stakeholders' expectations? If you answered "no" to any of these questions, whether you are the leader or a member of the group, you should explore the roots of the problems your group might be experiencing.

Do you have the right talent or resources in the group to get the job done? Is the group basing its work on faulty assumptions (e.g., what clients or customers value most, the promise of a new technology, the willingness of different agencies or divisions to cooperate)? Has something in your organization's environment changed, such as additional competition or new forms of regulation, making the group's original aims unrealistic or irrelevant?

Or, do you have a leadership problem?

The most common definition of a "leadership problem" is a "leader problem"—a problem stemming from the person or people in charge, such as managers, chairpersons, or team leaders. Are they not doing their jobs? How can they improve their effectiveness? Do they need to be replaced? It is reasonable to examine what the individuals with formal authority in the group are or are not doing that is contributing to the group not achieving results. However, the quick leap from "leadership problem" to "leader problem" can create tunnel vision.

Leadership involves far more than the person who holds the leader title. It is a *social process* that enables individuals to work together as a cohesive group to produce collective results—results they could never achieve working as individuals. Central to the process are the interactions and exchanges between the formal leader and group members, and among group members themselves. The process is influenced by the beliefs and values of the individuals involved, the quality of relationships in the group, formal structures and procedures, and the group's informal routines. To diagnose the source of problems in this process, one needs to take a *whole system* rather than an *individual leader* perspective. Formal leaders are an important part of the system, yet they are only one component in the multifaceted and dynamic process of leadership.

How do you assess the effectiveness of a group's leadership process? The most useful place to start is with the immediate outcomes that the leadership process needs to produce. When the leadership process in a group is effective, it generates three crucial outcomes: direction, alignment, and commitment (DAC).

DIRECTION is widespread agreement in the group on overall goals. In groups with strong direction, members have a shared understanding of what group success looks like and agree on what they are aiming to accomplish. In groups with weak direction, members are uncertain about what they should accomplish together, or they feel pulled in different directions by competing goals.

ALIGNMENT is coordinated work within the group. In groups with strong alignment, members with different tasks or roles or with different sets of expertise coordinate their work. In groups with weak alignment, members work more in isolation, unclear about how their tasks fit into the larger work of the group and are in danger of working at cross-purposes, duplicating effort, or having important work fall through the cracks.

COMMITMENT is mutual responsibility for the group. In groups with strong commitment, members feel responsible for the success and well-being of the group, and know that other group members feel the same. They trust one another and will stick with the group through difficult times. In groups with weak commitment, members put their own interests ahead of the group's interests and contribute to the group only when it is easy to do so or when they have something to gain.

3

DAC LEADERSHIP FRAMEWORK

LEADERSHIP PROCESS

INFLUENCES

- Beliefs & Values
- Quality of Relationships
- Formal Structures & Procedures
- Informal Routines

LEADERSHIP OUTCOMES

DIRECTION

ALIGNMENT

LEADERSHIP

COMMITMENT

GENERATES

IMPACTS

IMPACTS

RESULTS

OTHER FACTORS

• Marketplace Dynamics
• Available Resources
• Soundness of Business Strategy

Assessing the levels of DAC in your group and then examining potential contributing factors can help you diagnose what is not working in your current leadership process. It can help you see where you need to focus improvement efforts, and you can begin to explore ways of changing the group's leadership process so that it produces stronger DAC.

This book describes a three-step process for diagnosing DAC issues in groups:

1. Assess current levels of direction, alignment, and commitment in the group.
2. Look for factors contributing to low levels of direction, alignment, or commitment.
3. Identify changes that could improve direction, alignment, or commitment.

Before starting the diagnosis, here are a couple of important points to keep in mind:

- Although this three-step process asks you to examine direction, alignment, and commitment as independent outcomes, these leadership outcomes are interrelated. For example, having a widely agreed upon direction can enhance commitment to the group. Or, having group members strongly committed to the group can make alignment easier to achieve. While groups do find it useful to examine each outcome on its own, efforts to improve one outcome often have a spillover effect that impacts the other outcomes in positive ways.

- This process doesn't lead to an answer to your leadership problem; it doesn't point to a specific solution that will enhance direction or alignment or commitment. There are many possible solutions. What will work in one particular group depends on the individuals in the group, the group's work, and the larger context in which the group operates. However, careful diagnosis is an important and necessary starting point in resolving a leadership problem—one that increases your chances of investing in changes that will make a difference.

Not all group performance problems are DAC problems. Groups encounter other problems that keep them from achieving desired results, like unexpected changes in the external environment, unsound business practices, or limited resources. In these instances, strengthening DAC likely will not improve group performance. DAC is a determinant of group performance, but not the only determinant.

A DAC PROBLEM IMPACTING GROUP RESULTS	OTHER FACTORS IMPACTING GROUP RESULTS
Two years after starting a non-profit organization, founding members cannot agree on the organization's top priorities, making it difficult to attract financial support (direction problem).	A nonprofit organization has clear priorities, but a more established and visible organization takes on similar priorities and gains a larger share of funder resources (unexpected competitor problem).
Individuals on a product enhancement team don't coordinate their work well, resulting in rework and delays in updating the product (alignment problem).	An updated product is launched on time, but sales do not meet expectations because consumers see little added value in the new features (market research problem).
Task force members are more interested in using the forum to advance their personal agendas than in helping the group succeed, resulting in a set of recommendations that don't address some of the core problems they were asked to resolve (commitment problem).	Because task force members do not have all the expertise needed, they cannot successfully resolve the complex issue they were charged with (talent problem).

STEP 1:
ASSESS CURRENT LEVELS OF **DIRECTION**, ALIGNMENT, AND **COMMITMENT** IN THE GROUP

Let's start by examining three groups struggling with DAC outcomes.

The board of a state-focused foundation whose mission is to improve the health of its underprivileged citizens is creating a new five-year strategic plan. As the board evaluates the impact of the foundation's grants over the last five years, several board members express concerns that the foundation might be headed in the wrong direction. While some of the individual programs the foundation funds have resulted in impressive successes, the board hasn't seen enough improvement on overall health indicators for the underprivileged. Every board member supports the foundation's mission, and while the board feels good about what the foundation has achieved across the state, they wonder why the results don't reflect greater impact. Does the foundation's overall direction need to change radically to get the results they hope for? Some members seem eager to embrace a new direction; others are feeling the need to be more cautious.

Gabriela is serving on a cross-functional team designing and implementing an onboarding process for all new employees. Team members know what they are trying to achieve; they worked together to craft a team charter that everyone supports. They've put in place a plan to accomplish the work and assigned specific tasks to each team member. However, the team is falling behind its timelines and Gabriela is worried. Sometimes the team seems unclear about who is responsible for what, and they have to revisit and clarify assignments. She also has noticed that the team gets bogged down when trying to reconcile different ideas about how best to design some aspects of the overall process. She doesn't think the team has a direction problem, but are they struggling with aligning their work?

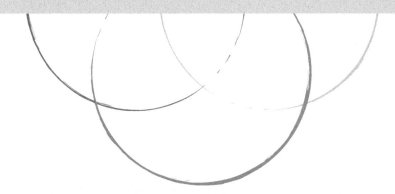

Deon is the project manager for a new product development team responsible for developing the next big innovation in the organization's most important product line. The team has extensive market research into customer needs, representatives from critical organization departments, and a substantial budget for prototyping and testing. Unfortunately, the team is experiencing extensive quality issues with the first prototype they sent to market testing. At each of their last three team meetings, at least 1–2 members have been absent due to schedule conflicts or competing deadlines. Since none of the team members report directly to Deon, he struggles with how to get the group to commit the time and effort required to address the quality issues so that the team can achieve its goals.

When you find yourself in similar situations, concerned about whether individuals are pulling together in ways needed to succeed as a group, it is time to step back and assess the degree to which the group has the DAC it needs. Use the statements in the following "DAC Assessment" to complete a systematic assessment of DAC in the group. Better yet, have everyone in the group rate each of the statements and combine answers. Getting this broader input from group members is particularly important if you are the formal leader of the group. Your position in the group can skew your perspective! For instance, you may be less likely to sense a direction problem because you had a hand in setting the direction.

DAC ASSESSMENT

Instructions: On a scale of 1-5, indicate the extent to which each of the following statements describes the way things stand right now in the group. The terms *we*, *our*, *everyone*, and *people* in the statements refer to members of the group. Once you've rated the individual statements, add up your ratings in each section to yield total scores for direction, alignment, and commitment.

This assessment is also available at **www.ccl.org/dac**.

1	**2**	**3**	**4**	**5**
Not Descriptive	Slightly Descriptive	Moderately Descriptive	Greatly Descriptive	Completely Descriptive

DIRECTION

1. We agree on what we should be aiming to accomplish together.	1	2	3	4	5
2. We have a clear vision of what the group needs to achieve in the future.	1	2	3	4	5
3. We understand what success looks like for this group.	1	2	3	4	5
4. We have group goals that guide our key decisions.	1	2	3	4	5
5. We have group priorities that help us focus on the most important work.	1	2	3	4	5
TOTAL					

ALIGNMENT

6. Our work is aligned across the group.	1	2	3	4	5
7. Although individuals take on different tasks in the group, our combined work fits together.	1	2	3	4	5
8. The work of each individual is well coordinated with the work of others.	1	2	3	4	5
9. People who perform different roles or functions coordinate their work effectively.	1	2	3	4	5
10. People are clear about how their tasks fit into the work of the group.	1	2	3	4	5
TOTAL					

COMMITMENT

11. People in the group are committed to the group.	1	2	3	4	5
12. We take responsibility for the welfare of the group.	1	2	3	4	5
13. We make the success of the group—not just our individual success—a priority.	1	2	3	4	5
14. People are dedicated to this group even when we face setbacks.	1	2	3	4	5
15. We put what is in the best interest of the group first.	1	2	3	4	5
TOTAL					

There are a number of ways to gather DAC assessment data from group members that keeps their identity anonymous (which encourages honest responses), and combines their data into a group-level summary for the entire group to review:

- Distribute paper copies of the assessment and have group members return it to a central person who tallies the data for the group.
- Create an online survey and send the link to group members. The survey package typically will produce a group summary of the data.
- Ask group members to complete the assessment and bring it to a group meeting. The assessment sheets can be gathered, shuffled, and randomly redistributed. Individuals can then transfer the data from the sheet they received to a wall chart that allows the group to see the whole group's data.

Group members can complete the assessment at www.ccl.org/dac and bring the printed results to a group meeting.

Whichever process you use, the goal of this assessment step is to identify whether any or all of the three key leadership outcomes is low in the group. Some criteria for deciding if an outcome is low include

- a total score for an outcome is noticeably lower than the total score for the other outcomes
- a total score for an outcome is less than 20
- two to three of the items used to assess an outcome are rated less than four by a majority of group members

If the group identifies one or more low outcomes, you should begin exploring what factors may be contributing to these deficits.

If you don't have time for everyone to do the assessment, here's an alternative for getting a quick read on DAC in the group. Provide the DAC diagram below with the short description of each outcome and have group members engage in a dot-voting exercise. Supply each group member with one each of two different colored sticky dots (small circular labels): one color (e.g., green) to vote for the group's strongest leadership outcome (direction, alignment, or commitment) and one color (e.g., red) to vote for the group's weakest leadership outcome. Have each group member write the letter (D, A, or C) on the colored dot representing the strongest element and likewise on the colored dot representing the weakest element. By writing the letter on the colored dot, each individual has to commit to his or her vote before seeing how others have voted. Then have each group member place their dots on the corresponding part of the diagram. As a group, discuss the outcome that gets the most "strongest" votes and the outcome that gets the most "weakest" votes and why they each think that is. Allow group members to provide the rationale for their vote.

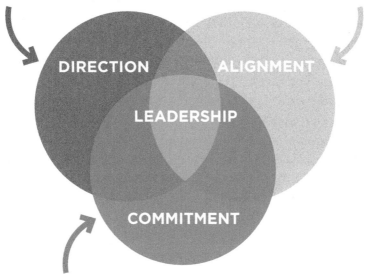

We agree on what we intend to accomplish together. We understand what success looks like for this group.

Although individuals take on different tasks in the group, our combined work fits together. The work of each individual is well coordinated with the work of others.

DIRECTION

ALIGNMENT

LEADERSHIP

COMMITMENT

We make the success of the group—not just our individual success—a priority. We take responsibility for the welfare of the group.

STEP 2:
LOOK FOR FACTORS CONTRIBUTING TO LOW LEVELS OF **DIRECTION**, ALIGNMENT, OR **COMMITMENT**.

What if your assessment of the group's direction, alignment, or commitment is low? Let's look at a number of contributing factors that might be at work.

DIRECTION PROBLEMS

As the board members discuss the foundation's future strategic direction, they discover points of disagreement. Some board members feel that to move the needle on key health indicators for underprivileged citizens, the foundation should invest in 1–3 key priority areas where they can work to create long-lasting change. Other board members have concerns about putting all of the foundation's assets into only a few key areas as they would have to sever relationships with many health-focused nonprofits in the community that provide much needed services. Would those organizations survive without the foundation's support? What if the key areas they invest in don't "pay off"?

Disagreement or concerns about a shared direction are common issues for groups, whether the groups are setting the direction for the entire organization (as with the foundation board), one department, or a particular project. If the stated and agreed upon direction is too broad, groups may interpret it in multiple ways that ultimately don't help guide their decisions or work. If a formal leader decides which specific direction the group will pursue without discussing the options or the rationale for that decision with other members of the group, will it be followed? Will this lack of direction lead to alignment and commitment issues down the road?

Use the Direction Issues Checklist to reflect on possible factors contributing to weak direction in your group.

DIRECTION ISSUES CHECKLIST

Check any of the factors below that could be contributing to weak direction on your team. Seek input from others to confirm your observations.

DIRECTION IS NOT CLEAR.

- ☐ We are in the early stages of working together and have not taken the time to articulate a shared direction.

- ☐ Many people assume there's a common direction, but we've never really talked about it.

- ☐ The individuals in charge decided on a direction, but others have not had an opportunity to discuss, digest, and really understand the direction.

THERE'S DISAGREEMENT ABOUT DIRECTION.

- ☐ We only agree on a very general direction, but it is so broad and nebulous that different people understand it in different ways.

- ☐ There's disagreement about the best direction, but it isn't openly acknowledged.

- ☐ We can't resolve our differences about the best direction to pursue, so we agree to disagree.

THERE'S RESISTANCE TO CREATING A SHARED DIRECTION.

- ☐ We fear choosing a shared direction because that one direction might end up being the wrong one.

- ☐ People aren't interested in combining efforts toward a shared direction; they want to work independently.

- ☐ Individuals are concerned that prioritizing work in service of a shared direction will eliminate or reduce the importance of tasks or projects they are currently engaged in.

15

ALIGNMENT PROBLEMS

Gabriela raised her concerns about the progress of the employee onboarding team with her team members. She found that others were also worried. Even though the team created a plan and assigned tasks appropriately, their ongoing coordination processes were weak. Individuals were completing tasks without communicating with others, often making assumptions that they didn't check with teammates. Without regular communication and sharing of ongoing work, team members failed to notice gaps in their work. And although the group had a task plan, they had not talked about how the group was going to work together, particularly when the group found themselves disagreeing. They had not taken into account that they were a cross-functional team coming from different departments in the organization, each of which had its own norms about teamwork.

Lack of clarity about responsibilities and weak coordination processes are two of the main factors that contribute to alignment issues in groups. Poor structuring of work, for example, by overloading certain team members or assigning work to individuals who don't have the needed skills, can also contribute to weak alignment. Coordination requires effort and time from team members. If coordination is not valued or rewarded, then it is less likely to happen.

Use the Alignment Issues Checklist to reflect on possible factors contributing to weak alignment in your group.

ALIGNMENT ISSUES CHECKLIST

Check any of the factors below that could be contributing to weak alignment on your team. Seek input from others to confirm your observations.

COORDINATION PROCESSES ARE WEAK.

☐ We jump into tasks and projects before putting together a plan for our work.

☐ Individuals don't see the bigger picture of how their work connects with other work.

☐ Individuals accomplish work on their own without communicating with others.

☐ Individuals don't involve others with relevant expertise.

☐ We don't have a system or process for effectively monitoring the work of the group as a whole.

STRUCTURING OF WORK IS POOR.

☐ All the tasks necessary for accomplishing the work of the group have not been clearly identified and resourced.

☐ Some people have too much work, some too little.

☐ Some people do not have the level of knowledge or skills needed to accomplish assigned work.

☐ Resources for accomplishing work are not appropriately allocated among group members.

Continued on page 18

Continued from page 17

ACCOUNTABILITIES/RESPONSIBILITIES ARE UNCLEAR.

☐ We haven't clearly articulated who is responsible for what tasks.

☐ Individuals do not know who has the authority to make what decisions.

☐ Individuals are not clear about what the group expects of them.

☐ There are aspects of the group's work that no one takes responsibility for, thus these aspects often fall through the cracks.

☐ There are conflicts among individuals over who is accountable for different aspects of the work.

☐ Individuals are unaware that others are doing the same or similar tasks, resulting in unnecessary duplication of effort.

☐ Individuals are not held accountable when they don't carry out assigned responsibilities.

THERE'S LOW MOTIVATION FOR COORDINATION.

☐ Individuals are not rewarded for coordinating with others.

☐ Coordinating with others is hard work, so people avoid doing it.

☐ Coordinating with others takes time away from a person's primary responsibilities, so they don't give it the attention it needs.

☐ People in positions of authority actively discourage coordination.

COMMITMENT PROBLEMS

In Deon's case, because the new product had the potential to be very successful and high profile (a possible new "cash-cow" for the organization), Deon thought everyone on the team was excited and equally committed to developing it. In reality, some of the team members have their own projects that they lead and for which they feel more ownership. They are not sure the organization will acknowledge or reward their contributions to this new product development team as much as they feel they will get rewarded for success in their own group's projects. They will do their share of the work but feel they can fit that work into their existing schedule with little regard to how their individual timelines affect other team members or the organization as a whole.

Self-interest at the expense of the group, and individuals not taking responsibility for the group as a whole, are two primary factors contributing to weak commitment. Most people have competing priorities for their time and effort. The culture of the organization or the norms for how the team decides to operate can also hinder or enable members' commitment level. Often projects that people are highly committed to at the outset encounter unexpected obstacles along the road to success or completion. These challenges can affect people's commitment or sense of responsibility to the team.

Use the Commitment Issues Checklist to reflect on possible factors contributing to weak commitment in your group.

COMMITMENT ISSUES CHECKLIST

Check any of the factors below that could be contributing to weak commitment on your team. Seek input from others to confirm your observations.

INDIVIDUALS DON'T FEEL RESPONSIBLE FOR THE GROUP.

☐ Individuals think of themselves as primarily doing individual work, not as group members with responsibility to the work of the whole group.

☐ Individuals complain about what's not working in the group but have no interest in fixing it.

☐ When obstacles or challenges get in the way of success, group members don't see themselves as having the ability or influence to address them.

☐ People are concerned that others may think they are greedy for responsibility if they take responsibility for something other than their own tasks.

MEMBERS DON'T SEE THEMSELVES AS PART OF THIS GROUP.

☐ The group is new, and people are still trying to get a sense of whether they want to commit to the group.

☐ There's constant turnover in group membership; it's hard to establish a sense of who the group really is.

☐ The group is made up of a number of small subgroups; individuals feel committed to those subgroups rather than to the group as a whole.

☐ There's a central powerful subgroup that dominates the group; other people feel left out.

☐ This group is just one more group that individuals are part of; it's not a meaningful group for most people.

MEMBERS DON'T VALUE BEING PART OF THIS GROUP.

- ☐ Individuals don't feel that they benefit from being part of this group.

- ☐ The work of the group is not engaging to some members.

- ☐ Relationships in the group are strained; individuals dislike working with one another.

- ☐ Individuals feel like they don't get the credit they deserve for their contributions to the group.

- ☐ The work of the group is not valued in the larger organization or community.

INDIVIDUALS ARE SELF-INTERESTED AT THE EXPENSE OF THE GROUP.

- ☐ Individuals publicly talk about supporting the group but privately pursue personal ends.

- ☐ Individuals take advantage of the group for their personal gain.

- ☐ The climate of the group is overly competitive; individuals argue for their own ideas and don't compromise with others

- ☐ Individuals frequently complain about how some aspect of the group process is a burden to them personally.

STEP 3:
IDENTIFY CHANGES THAT COULD IMPROVE **DIRECTION**, ALIGNMENT, OR **COMMITMENT**.

Once you've identified possible factors contributing to low levels of direction, alignment, or commitment in your group, you can begin to mitigate the factors and improve these outcomes. As to what specific changes your group should make, the answer will vary depending on a whole host of factors that distinguish it from other groups, including its size, the work it is engaged in, the degree of task interdependency in doing the work, what its members value, the organization it is embedded in, and the constraints and expectations imposed by that organization. A process for creating a clearer direction in one group might not work in another. The same is true for producing more highly coordinated work or for generating a stronger sense of responsibility for the group. There are no formulas for strengthening DAC; in fact, there are an infinite number of ways that DAC *might* be enhanced. You have to discover what works in your context.

INVOLVE GROUP MEMBERS
To maximize the probability of improving DAC, we recommend engaging group members in the process. Doing so not only provides a broader understanding of the dynamics of the situation but also makes their insights available for use in forming improvement strategies. You sought the group's input in Steps 1 and 2, and you can continue to involve group members by asking such questions as:

- What do we as a group see as the factors contributing to our DAC problem?

- What can we do to reduce or eliminate these factors?

- Which of these are most important to tackle first? What steps might we take to improve the situation?

- How might we evaluate the effectiveness of the actions we take?

- How often should we continue to assess the levels of DAC we are achieving?

SEEK OUT EXPERTISE

For any of the DAC issues that you uncover, there is a wealth of existing knowledge about how the issue can be addressed. For example, there are well-documented processes for articulating a shared vision, resolving conflicts within groups, coordinating work, creating clear accountability, building a strong team culture, and fostering a sense of responsibility for the group's success. We've included references at the end of this guidebook that will help you tap into that expertise. At the same time, don't discount the expertise that you've developed from your own experience. Reflect on what's worked in similar situations that could be applied to the current group. And look for benchmarking opportunities. Are there similar groups in the organization or community that have effectively dealt with the issue? What can you learn from them?

TAKE A SYSTEMS PERSPECTIVE

Keep in mind that direction, alignment, and commitment are *group-level* outcomes. Any aspect of the group can impact those outcomes. To enhance DAC, you might need to change the quality or frequency of interactions among group members, the relationships among particular members, the formal or informal processes for making decisions or getting work accomplished, the skills and motivation of individual group members, or the shared assumptions and cultural beliefs of the group as a whole. You should view the group as a DAC-producing system and examine all aspects of that system when exploring potential changes. Use the DAC system element list that follows to help determine what changes you need to make.

23

DAC SYSTEM ELEMENT LIST

Are changes in one or more of these system elements needed to enhance direction, alignment, or commitment in your group?

1. INDIVIDUAL GROUP MEMBERS' SKILLS AND MOTIVATION

a. Knowledge, skills, and abilities represented in the group
b. Personal values of group members
c. Extent to which individuals identify with the group
d. Engagement of individuals in the work of the group
e. Individual motivation to contribute to the group

2. GROUP COMPOSITION AND STRUCTURE

a. Size of group
b. Diversity of group members
c. Stability of group membership
d. Organization of the group into subgroups
e. Reporting relationships

3. INTERACTIONS AMONG GROUP MEMBERS

a. Communication patterns (i.e., who communicates with whom, about what, how frequently)
b. Type of access group members have to one another
c. Frequency and quality of group meetings
d. Customary ways of treating one another
e. Typical strategies for dealing with conflict

4. RELATIONSHIPS IN THE GROUP

a. How well group members know each other
b. Level of trust among group members
c. Structure of informal networks in the groups
d. Presence of any strained relationships in the group
e. Relationship of formal leader with group members

5. GROUP PROCESSES

    a. Planning processes

    b. How work is assigned

    c. How work is accomplished

    d. Performance management processes

    e. Decision-making processes

    f. Information-sharing practices

    g. Processes for developing group members

    h. Reward systems

6. GROUP CULTURE

    a. Shared beliefs about what's important

    b. Informal rules of behavior in the group

    c. Assumptions about what is right or true

    d. Values that group members aspire to

    e. Traditions maintained by the group

7. RELATIONSHIP WITH EXTERNAL ENVIRONMENT

    a. Quality of relationships with key stakeholders

    b. Degree of isolation or connection with larger community

    c. External processes and regulations governing the group

    d. Openness to external influence

    e. Reputation of group in larger organization or community

ENGAGE IN A CONTINUOUS LEARNING PROCESS

You won't know if a change is going to yield the desired outcomes until you try it. You'll benefit the most from these change experiments if you are clear about what you expect to improve as a result of the change, regularly evaluate whether those improvements are achieved (and monitor any unintended effects of the changes), and make adjustments based on what you learn. The After-Action Review activity below is one tool that can help you monitor the impact of changes made to the leadership process.

AFTER-ACTION REVIEW

After-Action Reviews can help a group reflect on whether a change they are attempting is improving their leadership process in desired ways, what they are learning from their efforts to improve, and what additional changes they may need to make.

STEP 1

After the group has experimented with an intentional change in some aspect of their leadership process, recreate the following chart on a flip chart, white board, or piece of paper:

INTENDED	ACTUAL
LESSONS	**DO SAME/DO DIFFERENTLY**

STEP 2

Through a facilitated discussion, invite team members to reflect on their work and consider

- What did we intend to do? (Intended)
- What actually happened? (Actual)
- What did we learn? (Lessons)
- What will we do the same or differently to be more effective in the future? (Do Same/Do Differently)

STEP 3

Capture the ideas that emerge from the group on the chart.

OPTIONS

- An alternative approach is to ask team members to reflect on these questions privately, and jot their responses on a sticky-note—one note per question.
- The facilitator then talks through what is on the notes and encourages discussion among group or team members.

THE REST OF
THE STORY

Each of our groups explored options for dealing with the particular leadership problem they had uncovered and experimented with new leadership practices to see what worked best in their specific situation.

To help understand and explore the pros and cons of radically shifting the foundation's strategic direction, the board established a subcommittee comprising a few board members and senior leadership from the foundation staff. The subcommittee examined what other foundations that made major strategic shifts in direction had done and what they had learned. The subcommittee also spent time talking with different community leaders engaged in improving the health of state citizens. After sharing what they learned with the full board, the subcommittee arranged for an outside facilitator to guide the board through a strategic planning session to assess and determine the best course of action. Ultimately the board decided to make a major shift in how the foundation's assets were invested and to focus on a few key strategies that the board felt would lead to longer lasting, higher impact changes and improve the health of the state's citizens. Shifting the foundation toward that end required a systemic view of the current problem as well as the opportunities for improvements. It also necessitated multiple conversations with the foundation staff and many of their long-standing grantees so that they understood and shared the new direction.

Borrowing from their past experiences with effective teams, the employee onboarding team experimented with new coordination and monitoring processes. Those experiments helped the team identify interdependencies in their work that needed closer coordination, added more frequent update check-ins, and created a shared workspace so that in-process work products could be viewed by anyone on the team. To help members make better decisions when they disagreed, the team created a quick process for summarizing the pros and cons of alternative choices. Members decided that if they still couldn't agree, they would ask the formal team leader to arbitrate. The final change the team made was to be more intentional about getting to know each other as people. Because members came from different parts of the organization, they had very little interaction before the project started. They built in more time for relationship building during meetings, and they took on some of the work in pairs to capitalize on the rapport that can come from working closely with another person. This new focus led to increased team coordination. As the team reviewed their performance and learning at their final meeting, they realized that their efforts to achieve more aligned work had also enhanced their commitment to the group.

Deon called an "emergency meeting" for all team members so they could discuss the extensive quality problems with the first prototype. So as not to put any one team member on the spot, Deon facilitated the team in an After-Action Review process so they could individually and collectively assess the things that did not go as planned and what they could do differently to ensure higher quality. He asked the team's members to reflect on the challenges they were encountering when it came to attending planned team meetings or meeting crucial deadlines. With those thoughts in hand, team members were able to brainstorm ways to better support each other in the "do differently" part of the discussion. By acknowledging and validating the obstacles some individual members (as well as the team) were facing and brain-storming ways to help each other overcome those obstacles, they were able to renew their commitment to the team. They began to talk more openly and support each other when other priorities or challenges threatened to disrupt their progress. The team incor-porated regular check-in conversations to respond to any indi-vidual team member's challenges that occurred during the team's product-development work.

By examining leadership as a social process that produces three critical outcomes—direction, alignment, and commitment—group members have the opportunity to diagnose and address factors inhibiting their ability to work together as a cohesive group to produce collective results. The key is to start by identi-fying which of these outcomes is lacking and what might be con-tributing to the deficit. A solid diagnosis is at the foundation of redesigning and experimenting with an improved leadership pro-cess. Although formal leaders might feel particularly compelled to find ways to improve DAC in the groups they are responsible for, *everyone* can play an important role in calling attention to and resolving DAC issues in the groups in which they participate.

BACKGROUND

The beginnings of the DAC leadership framework emerged more than 15 years ago as CCL explored new directions in the understanding and development of leadership. Historically, CCL recognized leadership as essentially an interpersonal influence process. Leadership was about individuals (called leaders) influencing other people (called followers) to engage in the pursuit of shared goals. This asymmetrical influence relationship is at the heart of most traditional leadership theories.

The DAC framework was influenced by a constructivist and relational view of leadership (Drath & Palus, 1994; Drath, 2001) and a leadership development practice that was broadening beyond CCL's original focus on individuals to include the development of leadership systems in organizations (O'Connor & Quinn, 2004). A core question was "What does it take for individuals to willingly and effectively combine their efforts to produce collective results?" Knowledge gleaned from research, theory, and experience pointed to three key ingredients: a shared direction, alignment of work, and commitment to the collective. This outcome-focused perspective on the essential elements of leadership represented a departure from traditional conceptualizations (Drath, McCauley, Palus, Van Velsor, O'Connor, & McGuire, 2008) and became a foundational element of CCL's leadership development practice (Van Velsor, McCauley, & Ruderman, 2010).

We use the DAC framework in many different contexts—in the classroom, as we coach teams, when we work with organizations on change initiatives, as we help communities build collaborative networks, and in our leadership research. We use it with diverse people across sectors and around the world. As people try on this way of thinking about leadership and share their experiences with us, we continue to refine and deepen our understanding of what it takes to make leadership happen.

SUGGESTED RESOURCES

DIRECTION

Cartwright, T., & Baldwin, D. (2006). *Communicating your vision.* Greensboro, NC: Center for Creative Leadership.

Center for Creative Leadership. Self-paced course—Creating a vision. E-course retrieved from http://solutions.ccl.org/Self-Paced-Course-Creating-a-Vision.

Hughes, R. L., Beatty, K. C., & Dinwoodie, D. L. (2014). *Becoming a strategic leader: Your role in your organization's enduring success.* San Francisco, CA: John Wiley and Sons.

Kanaga, K., & Kossler, M. E. (2001). *How to form a team: Five keys to high performance.* Greensboro, NC: Center for Creative Leadership.

Kanaga, K., & Prestridge, S. (2002). *How to launch a team: Start right for success.* Greensboro, NC: Center for Creative Leadership.

Kania, J., & Kramer, M. (2011). Collective impact. *Stanford Social Innovation Review, 9*(1), 36–41.

Weisbord, M. R. (1992). *Discovering common ground: How future search conferences bring people together to achieve breakthrough innovation, empowerment, shared vision, and collaborative action.* San Francisco, CA: Berrett-Kohler Publishers.

ALIGNMENT

Cartwright, T. (2003). *Managing conflict with peers.* Greensboro, NC: Center for Creative Leadership.

Kanaga, K., & Browning, H. (2003). *Maintaining team performance.* Greensboro, NC: Center for Creative Leadership.

Kanaga, K., & Kossler, M. E. (2001). *How to form a team: Five keys to high performance.* Greensboro, NC: Center for Creative Leadership.

Kanaga, K., & Prestridge, S. (2002). *How to launch a team: Start right for success.* Greensboro, NC: Center for Creative Leadership.

Kania, J., & Kramer, M. (2011). Collective impact. *Stanford Social Innovation Review, 9*(1), 36–41.

Project Management Institute. (2013). *A guide to the project management body of knowledge.* Newtown Square, PA: Author.

Turregano, C. (2013). *Delegating effectively: A leader's guide to getting things done.* Greensboro, NC: Center for Creative Leadership.

COMMITMENT

Bunker, K. (2008). *Responses to change: Helping people manage transition.* Greensboro, NC: Center for Creative Leadership.

Browning, H. (2012). *Accountability: Taking ownership of your responsibility.* Greensboro, NC: Center for Creative Leadership.

Cartwright, T. (2003). *Managing conflict with peers.* Greensboro, NC: Center for Creative Leadership.

Druskat, V. U., & Wolff, S. B. (2003). Building the emotional intelligence of groups. *Harvard Business Review, 79*(3), 80–90.

Hoppe, M. H. (2006). *Active listening: Improve your ability to listen and lead.* Greensboro, NC: Center for Creative Leadership.

Kaye, B. L. (1999). *Love 'em or lose 'em: Getting good people to stay.* San Francisco, CA: Berrett-Koehler Publishers.

Kirkland, K., & Manoogian, S. (1998). *Ongoing feedback: How to get it, how to use it.* Greensboro, NC: Center for Creative Leadership.

Klann, G. (2004). *Building your team's morale, pride, and spirit.* Greensboro, NC: Center for Creative Leadership.

Reina, D., & Reina, M. (2010). *Rebuilding trust in the workplace: Seven steps to renew confidence, commitment, and energy.* San Francisco, CA: Berrett-Koehler Publishers.

ADDITIONAL RESOURCES

Drath, W. (2001). *The deep blue sea: Rethinking the source of leadership.* San Francisco, CA: Jossey-Bass.

Drath, W. H., & Palus, C. J. (1994). *Making common sense: Leadership as meaning-making in a community of practice.* Greensboro, NC: Center for Creative Leadership.

Drath, W. H., McCauley, C. D., Palus, C. J., Van Velsor, E., O'Connor, P.M.G., & McGuire, J. B. (2008). Direction, alignment, commitment: Toward a more integrative ontology of leadership. *The Leadership Quarterly,* 19, 635-63.

O'Connor, P.M.G., & Quinn, L. (2004). Organizational capacity for leadership. In C.D. McCauley & E. Van Velsor (Eds.), *The Center for Creative Leadership handbook of leadership development* (2nd edition). San Francisco, CA: Jossey-Bass.

Van Velsor, E., McCauley, C. D., & Ruderman, M. N. (Eds.) (2010). *The Center for Creative Leadership handbook of leadership development* (3rd edition). San Francisco, CA: Jossey-Bass.

NOTES

ABOUT THE CENTER FOR CREATIVE LEADERSHIP

The Center for Creative Leadership (CCL) is a top-ranked, global provider of leadership development. By leveraging the power of leadership to drive results that matter most to clients, CCL transforms individual leaders, teams, organizations, and society. Our array of cutting-edge solutions is steeped in extensive research and experience gained from working with hundreds of thousands of leaders at all levels. Ranked among the world's Top 5 providers of executive education by *Financial Times* and in the Top 10 by *Bloomberg BusinessWeek*, CCL has offices in Greensboro, NC; Colorado Springs, CO; San Diego, CA; Brussels, Belgium; Moscow, Russia; Addis Ababa, Ethiopia; Johannesburg, South Africa; Singapore; Gurgaon, India; and Shanghai, China.

IDEAS
INTO
ACTION

ORDERING INFORMATION

To get more information, to order other books in the Ideas
Into Action Series, or to find out about bulk-order discounts,
please contact us by phone at 336-545-2810 or visit our
online bookstore at www.ccl.org/Leadership/books.